Ceciel de Bie
Martijn Leenen

Rembrandt

SEE AND DO CHILDREN'S BOOK

The J. Paul Getty Museum, Los Angeles

Daily life in Rembrandt's time

eating

playing in the street

playing on the swing

the tooth puller

the Amsterdam fish market

the notary

We would like to thank Michiel Franken and Sjaar van Heugten for their help in making this book, and everyone else who was involved with the book.

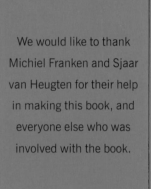
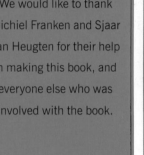

the laundry

the Amsterdam Stock Exchange

playing with a slingsh

© 1999 V+K Publishing, Blaricum, the Netherlands
Rembrandt, See and Do Children's Book
© 1999 Ceciel de Bie en Martijn Leenen, Amsterdam

First published in 2001 in the United States of America by:
The J. Paul Getty Museum
1200 Getty Center Drive, Suite 1000
Los Angeles, California 90049-1687
www.getty.edu/publications

ISBN 0-89236-621-4
Library of Congress Control Number: 2001087774

the smoking room

an Amsterdam cana

the spinner

the butcher

the ball game

What's in this book?

the street

the coach

the doctor

throwing a ball

flying a kite

hopscotch

bowling a hoop

fashion

In Search of Rembrandt

Have you ever heard of Rembrandt? The world-famous painter who lived four centuries ago? To this day, people from all over the world come to look at his paintings. His paintings make you curious. Who was Rembrandt really? And what was it like to live when he did? Shall we go in search of Rembrandt?

*I*t was the middle of summer when Rembrandt Harmensz van Rijn was born in Leiden in Holland on 15 July 1606. The Van Rijns were a big family. Rembrandt had eight brothers and sisters. His father owned a mill on the banks of the Old River Rhine. The mill was called 'De Rijn', which is Dutch for the Rhine, and that's how Rembrandt got his last name. The mill ground malt and malt is used to make beer. Beer was a popular drink then, so Rembrandt's father had a successful business.

Little Rembrandt was always drawing. Everyone praised him. 'That a young lad can make such beautiful drawings!' People never stopped talking about him. It came as no surprise that Rembrandt only wanted to be one thing - he wanted to be a painter.

Fortunately, his parents understood Rembrandt well. When he was thirteen, they went to look for a good teacher for him. One day, they met the painter Jacob van Swanenburgh. The teacher was very pleased with his pupil. Rembrandt was eager to learn and never stopped asking questions. After three years, Jacob couldn't teach him anything new. It was time for Rembrandt to find another teacher.

What Rembrandt really wanted was to go to Amsterdam and continue his studies with the famous painter Pieter Lastman. His father thought it was a good idea too. Pieter Lastman had been to Italy and was very enthusiastic about the bright colors used by the Italian painters. They often painted directly onto the walls of Italy's enormous palaces and buildings. Nobody had painted such big pictures in the Netherlands.

Pieter's enthusiastic stories made a great impression on Rembrandt. He also wanted to paint the way the Italian painters did.

In 1624, six months later, Rembrandt returned to Leiden. He had learned so much that he was able to start his own studio. The only thing on Rembrandt's mind was painting, just like his friend Jan Lievens. The two boys were always talking about it. But… they also kept a close eye on each other, because they both wanted to be the best.

One day, they heard that an important man wanted to come and visit them. It was Constantijn Huygens, who was a great admirer of art. They were very excited but also a little nervous. Would he like their work? Maybe they would get a big commission from him.

Constantijn Huygens was very impressed with their work. He wrote, 'They're more like children than young men but they are both very talented. I think Rembrandt is the best. He really shows people's feelings in his paintings in a way I've never seen before. Jan Lievens paints with a lot of confidence, on life-size canvases. There's one thing though – it's a pity they think they don't have the time to go to Italy themselves. They could learn so much from the Italian painters. They're only interested in painting. I've never met such industrious boys before. These pale-faced boys seem like old men, and they do nothing but paint.'

The name 'Rembrandt'

When a painter finishes a painting he puts his name on it. Not many people were called Rembrandt – it was an unusual first name. So he used the name Rembrandt to sign his work.

The studio

The Hague

The distance from Leiden to The Hague is about 17 miles. That's a five-hour walk.

Leiden

The Young Painter in His Studio (1626)

Rembrandt is working in his studio. This was probably a room on the first floor of his house in Leiden. It's not a new house. There are cracks in the plaster on the walls. In some places you can even see the bare bricks.

Rembrandt is wearing a long blue-gray painter's coat. He is looking at the panel on the easel. We can't see the front of the panel, but Rembrandt can. Has he started painting yet? Or is he still thinking about what he's going to paint?

Rembrandt is standing as far away as possible from the easel. That way he can see the whole panel. You can see Rembrandt from head to foot. He was the first painter to portray himself like that. Painters were always seated at their easel. They rested their feet on the bottom crossbar. Can you see where the crossbar has been worn away by the painter's feet?

In his right hand he is holding a paintbrush, ready to start painting. In his other hand he is holding more brushes and a long stick with a small, soft ball on the end. This is a painter's stick. He uses it for making very fine strokes. Carefully he presses the little ball against the panel and then he rests his hand on the stick. This stops his hand from shaking when he paints.

Two palettes are hanging on the wall. They are thin pieces of wood with a hole in them. If you stick your thumb through the hole, it helps you hold the palette properly. You put paint on the pallet. It makes it easier to mix the colors. On the tree stump next to the table is a grindstone. Painters often made their own paint. You could also buy ready-made paint. The paint was kept in pig bladders because tubes hadn't been invented yet.

How old is Rembrandt in the painting?

How can you tell that Rembrandt can put small and large panels on his easel?

Can you see what the floor is made of?

What can you see on the table?

Why do you think he is wearing a painter's coat?

Can you see where Rembrandt came into the studio?

Fifty years after Rembrandt's death, around 1720, the painter Arnold Houbraken wrote about Rembrandt's life. He never met Rembrandt himself. But he spoke to painters who had been pupils of Rembrandt. This book tells some of his stories about Rembrandt that he was told by Rembrandt's former pupils.

Houbraken recounts: A vague story

Rembrandt had just finished a drawing when he was visited by a friend. 'What a nice drawing,' said his friend. 'I know someone in The Hague you must show it to.' Rembrandt was keen to make some extra money. The next day he got up early to walk from Leiden to The Hague.

Rembrandt was paid a hundred guilders for his drawing! He was very pleased. He wanted to tell his parents as soon as possible. With all that money in his pocket, he of course didn't walk back home. He took the coach back to Leiden. On the way, the coach stopped at an inn to rest and feed the horses. Everyone got off to have a drink. Everyone except Rembrandt. He was scared that someone might steal his money. After a while, the other passengers and the coach driver came back. But before they could get on board, the horses bolted. They galloped all the way home. They only stopped when they had reached their stables in the city. People were surprised and asked Rembrandt what had happened. He told them a vague story and quickly disappeared. He grinned, he was pleased with himself. He had never traveled from The Hague to Leiden that fast, and it hadn't cost him a penny.

This is how paint was made

The colors in paint were made from ground-up stone, charcoal or plants. These colors were called pigments. In order to make the pigments even finer, they were ground on a grindstone. Then the pigments were mixed with oil. That's why it's called oil paint.

Amsterdam

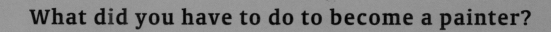

What did you have to do to become a painter?

*I*f you wanted to become a painter, you went into apprenticeship with a master painter. You could do this when you were ten. You went to live with him for a while. You worked in his studio together with other pupils. You started by copying pictures from a book. You had to practice endlessly. Hundreds of eyes, noses, mouths and all from different angles. If there was something wrong with your drawing, the master could see it straight away. Then he would explain how you could correct your mistake. When you had learned how to draw properly, you were allowed to start copying prints and paintings. You also drew studies of plaster sculptures. You learned how to make paint and prepare canvases. And, of course, as the youngest apprentice, you were given all the nasty jobs to do.

After a number of years, when you had learned enough about painting, you were made an assistant. To become a master painter yourself, you chose a master you admired very much. You could continue learning and also earn some money in his studio. You helped him with his paintings or you copied them. They had to be so good that it seemed that the master had painted them himself. And sometimes you were given an empty canvas. Then you were finally allowed to choose your subject and paint it for yourself. This gave you the chance to show whether you were good enough to become a master painter yourself.

Rembrandt's studio was a little bit different

Rembrandt didn't want his students to help him with his paintings. He preferred to paint them himself. The copies had to be good but his assistants were also allowed to try out their own ideas.

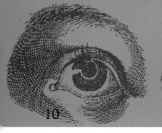

An artist's studio at the start of the 17th century

Fire hazard

There was no electric light. And working by candlelight was strictly forbidden. It was much too dangerous, with all those wooden buildings in the city. That's why you could only work in daylight, from sunrise to sunset. You finished work when you heard the evening bell.

Practice, practice, practice

You will need: pencil, paper and an eraser.
Ask someone to sit on a chair for you.
Take a good look at their eyes, nose and mouth.
See if you can draw them.

Off to Amsterdam

Rembrandt started to get so many commissions from Amsterdam that he decided to move there. His friend Hendrick van Uylenburgh invited him to live and work at his house. Hendrick had an art shop and a school for painters, but he couldn't paint himself. So he asked Rembrandt to teach at his school. In those days, paintings and copies of masterpieces were very popular. Assistants churned them out one after another. They sold like hotcakes. Rembrandt's own paintings were copied there as well. Rembrandt worked very hard. In the space of four years, he painted as many as fifty portraits!

Let's go back in time!

Imagine you could travel back in time… It's four hundred years ago. You're on your way by boat to the big city of Amsterdam for the very first time. Your dream has come true - you're going to be one of Rembrandt's assistants.

As you sail past the miles and miles of landing stages, you can see Amsterdam in the distance. Some really big ships are moored in the deepest part of the harbor. On the quays, stevedores are going back and forth carrying heavy sacks. Merchants are watching to make sure all the goods come ashore. As you sail into the city, you see a forest of masts and flags. The water is crowded with small boats. You continue sailing until you reach the Damrak, the place where small ships are unloaded. This is where you get off. As you walk along

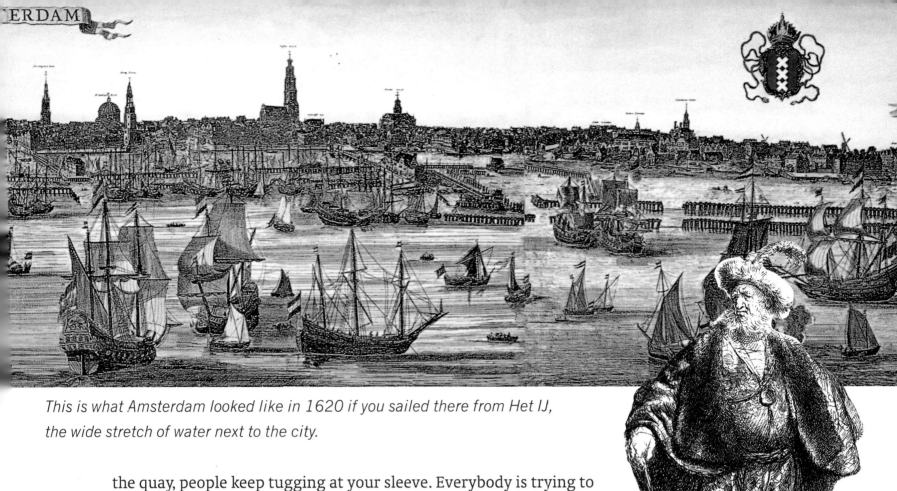

This is what Amsterdam looked like in 1620 if you sailed there from Het IJ, the wide stretch of water next to the city.

the quay, people keep tugging at your sleeve. Everybody is trying to sell you something. You look around in amazement. You've never seen so many different people. Merchants, elegantly dressed ladies and gentlemen, beggars, quack doctors, street musicians and foreigners wearing strange clothes.

Wandering through the alleyways, you peer into dark workshops. Chickens and goats are running around loose all over the place. Pigs are snuffling around in piles of rubbish. What a lot of noise and what an awful smell everywhere!

It's starting to rain. You dive into a building to take shelter. You find yourself in a big courtyard with pillars around it. 'This is the Commodity Exchange,' someone tells you. Merchants are all shouting about how good their wares are. At each pillar you can buy something different. Goods have been brought here from all over the world. This is the place to borrow money, too. If you want one, you can even buy a tiger here!

You're tired from your long journey and after your first day in Amsterdam. You start looking for somewhere to stay the night. You find a small inn and are given a straw mattress to sleep on. The sun has set. You hear a bell in the distance. It's the log bell. It means that logs will be lowered into the water so that no boats can enter the city at night. No one is allowed to enter or leave the city.

Tomorrow morning you're expected at Rembrandt's studio… It's difficult to fall asleep.

Rembrandt liked to make drawings or etchings of people he saw in the street.

13

The Amsterdam Times

Epidemic in working-class district

A cholera epidemic has broken out among the poor people of the city. Many have already died of the disease. It is spreading fast on the outskirts of the city. The working-class district, with its untidy workshops, dirty hovels and pigsties has suffered most. The disease is very infectious. So be warned, don't go there!

Now going cheap TULIP BULBS

In beautiful colors:
1 tulip bulb costs 7 bushels of wheat or 2 bushels of rice or 4 cows or 8 pigs. Come to pillar 298 at the Commodity Exchange.

New record - Three times as many inhabitants

In 1600, Amsterdam had only 50,000 inhabitants. Now, in 1650, this number has risen to 150,000.

The 'Hasewint' is a good example of a flute

New breakthrough with invention of 'flute'

Trade in Amsterdam is booming. At first, everybody laughed at the new 'flute' sailing ship because it looked so different. They refused to believe this new design would offer so many advantages. The 'flute' can carry a huge cargo across the sea. It is the biggest and fastest type of ship ever built. It is also very easy to navigate. It only needs a crew of ten men. Other ships need a crew of at least thirty. A real money-saver!

World's first newspaper

(1618) Amsterdam is the first city in the world to have a regular newspaper. What can you read about in the newspaper? The latest news on harvests in distant countries. Where the fleets are sailing. What things cost. And important information about the city itself.

Tailor gets caught

A tailor from Hatter's Alley has been caught working by candlelight. The man should have known better. Three years ago, a huge fire broke out in the alley. It was started by a candle used for working after dark. The man has been fined.

Piet Heijn's Silver Fleet coming

(1628) Our great sea hero Piet Heijn will sail into Amsterdam tomorrow with the Silver Fleet. Last September, he captured the Silver Fleet from the Spaniards in the Bay of Matanzas. The loot consisted of 177,000 pounds of silver, 66 pounds of gold, 1,000 pearls, 3 tons of silk, 37,375 hides and many more valuable goods.

Amsterdam - Europe's main trading city

Amsterdam is praised by neighboring countries as the best city for doing business. This is not so surprising. The people of Amsterdam have always been energetic and clever traders. The city's direct link with the sea makes it easily accessible. And to make it even easier for ships to come to Amsterdam, the harbors have been greatly extended. Amsterdam is now the obvious choice for sea traders looking for a place to unload their goods. In 1606, Amsterdam became the first city in Europe to have a bank of exchange. Here you can exchange coins from any other city or country for the currency of Amsterdam, the banco florin. It is the accepted currency in the city. Amsterdam not only attracts merchants but also painters, poets and scientists, who come here from all over the world to meet each other. As a result, it is a place where people think up all sorts of new ideas and opportunities.

Announcement: Crew wanted for new ship

On 10 April, a ship of the United East Indies Company will sail for the Cape of Good Hope. The Company is looking for a number of strong sailors and a cook. Sea-legs and a strong stomach are essential. Sign up at the Shipping Office at the harbor.

Digging of new canals started

Amsterdam in about 1650, when the canals are finished.

(1613) Because the population of Amsterdam has grown so fast in recent years, the city has become too small. Now the Council has come up with a brilliant plan to solve the problem. Three new canals will be dug in a semicircle around the city moat – The Gentlemen's Canal, The Emperor's Canal and the Prince's Canal. Space will be left between the canals to build houses on. Digging began yesterday when Captain Banning Cocq fired a shot to start the work.

Thousands of men started digging immediately. It will take years before this huge project is finished. The areas between the canals will be leveled with sand. To keep the building site dry, the water must be pumped out 24 hours a day. Thousands of piles will be needed to reinforce the banks of the canals. Many bridges will be built across the new waterways. Only when this work has been done can the building of houses start. Only wealthier citizens of Amsterdam will be able to buy the beautiful new canal houses, because the houses will not be cheap.

Beggars in the Street (1648), etching by Rembrandt

Too many beggars

From now on, beggars without a licence to beg will be arrested. Male beggars will be locked up in the Shredding House. As punishment they will have to shred wood. The women will go to the Spinning House where they will have to spin wool and weave cloth.

Never shown before

Come to the big tent on the Dam. Hanske the elephant from Ceylon has arrived in Amsterdam for the first time. This enormous animal will show tricks here she has never shown before. You will have a chance to see this spectacle until Sunday. Then Hanske will be taken on tour throughout Europe. Admission: 5 cents.

Hanske the Elephant (1637), drawing by Rembrandt.

The Syndics reject big lot of woolen cloth

Yesterday, the Syndics discovered serious flaws in woolen fabrics. The fabrics were not coloured an even blue. They had to reject twenty rolls of cloth. The merchant who was having his cloth inspected had overlooked the flaws. The cloth will be burned.

Significant loss

A fleet of five ships on their way home was caught in a heavy storm. Four ships have gone down with all hands.

Aid for hungry street children

During this extremely cold winter our fisherwomen have again seen to it that hungry street children have had enough to eat.

6 group portraits for the Amsterdam Militia Company

(1640) The clubhouse of our Militia Company has become too small. That's why the Militia Company has had a new banqueting hall built. They want to adorn the new hall with six group portraits. Six famous painters have been selected for this great commission: Jacob Adriaensz Backer, Govert Flinck, Bartholomeus van der Helst, Nicholaes Eliasz Pickenoy, Rembrandt van Rijn and Joachim von Sandrart.

The rich of Amsterdam

The rich in 1631
There are 4,000 wealthy citizens who live in Amsterdam. They each own more than 1,000 guilders.

Richer
About 100 Amsterdam citizens own more than 100,000 guilders.

Richest
But the richest man in Amsterdam is the merchant Jacob Poppen. He owns more than 500,000 guilders!

Hurricane destroys crop in Indonesia

A tropical hurricane raged over the plantations near Batavia yesterday. The harvest of precious spices, cinnamon, cloves, mace and nutmeg has unfortunately been destroyed.

Portraits

As if they could just step out of the painting

Rembrandt lived in an exceptional time, a time in which many people became very rich. That is why the seventeenth century is often called the Golden Age. The rich thought they were very important. They wanted to show this off to other people. So they had themselves portrayed in their finest clothes.

The photograph had not yet been invented. If you wanted a portrait you went to a painter. That's why people went to Rembrandt. The news spread like wildfire across Amsterdam that Rembrandt's portraits were very lifelike. It was as though the people in his portraits could just step out of the painting and start talking to you at any moment. Everyone wanted such a beautiful portrait. Rembrandt became busier and busier.

Rembrandt never simply just painted someone. He was always curious about the people he was going to paint. Was his subject a kind man, a strict woman, a naughty child or a dreamer? He wished he could read their thoughts. He thought that simply painting a true likeness was boring. Rembrandt wanted to show what people were really like in their daily lives.

Does Nicolaes look serious, angry, cheerful or friendly?

Is Nicolaes looking straight at you?

What is his right hand resting on?

Portrait of Nicolaes Ruts (1631)

This portrait of Nicolaes Ruts (1573-1638) was painted by Rembrandt. He was a rich Amsterdam merchant who traded with Russia. Russia can be very cold in the winter. That's why he is wearing a fur hat and a heavy coat.

What can you see that tells you Nicolaes is a rich man?

In the family for more than three hundred years

The art lover Jan Six was one of Rembrandt's friends. The painting shows him putting on his gloves. He is on the point of leaving. His red cape is loosely draped around his shoulders. His clothes are painted in broad brushstrokes but his kind face is painted in fine strokes.

The painting has been hanging in the Sixes' family home for more than three hundred years. And Jan Six still hasn't left yet ...

Painted in fine brushstrokes

Painted in broad brushstrokes

Portrait of Jan Six (1654) He lived from 1618 until 1700.

You could have your portrait painted in various ways:

Only your head and shoulders,

or only the top half of your body…

or from head to toe… This full-length portrait was the most expensive one.

Thick brushstrokes

Rembrandt's free manner of painting struck people as very unusual! In the paintings of most other painters you could hardly see the brushstrokes at all. In Rembrandt's paintings you could – and people weren't used to that. But they still found his paintings very beautiful. That was because Rembrandt was able to paint a glove or a coat, for instance, with only a few thick, free strokes – just like that!

Houbraken recounts: Monkey business

Rembrandt was painting a portrait of a father, a mother and their children. The painting was nearly finished when their favorite pet, a monkey, died. He wanted to paint a portrait of the monkey to remember it by. But he had no more canvas left. So he painted the monkey next to the family in the portrait. This made the family very angry. They did not want to be immortalized in a picture with such an ugly animal. But Rembrandt didn't even think once about painting over the monkey, he kept it in. And so the family didn't want the painting.

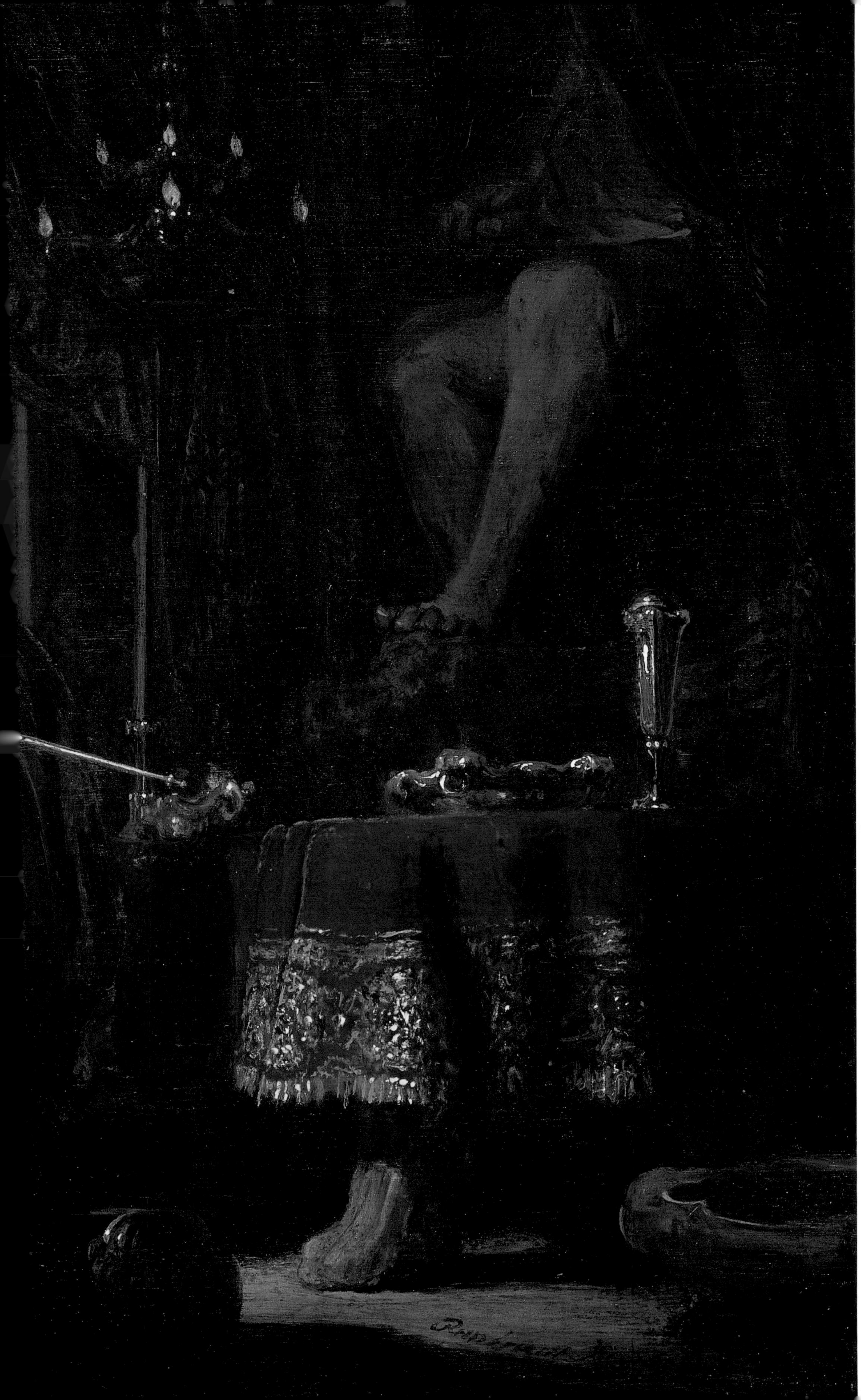

Able to paint anything

Happiest painting historical paintings

How does Rembrandt show who is the King?

Rembrandt's greatest wish was to be a good historical painter. A historical painter chooses a story from the Bible, or from history, or a story about the Greek or Roman gods. The painter uses them as subjects for his paintings. A historical painter has to be able to paint anything: people, animals and landscapes.

Rembrandt loved to read stories about faraway places although he never visited them himself. Luckily, he had a large collection of prints by other masters. When he had chosen a story, he selected prints to help him imagine what it was like in foreign countries. He was always looking for exotic clothes and rich and colorful materials for his models to wear. He was very particular about this. He once took two days to get the folds in a turban exactly right.

Where is the food and wine for the statue placed?

Can you see one of the priests in the painting?

Daniel and Cyrus Before the Idol Bel (1633), a story from the Bible

Daniel is a writer at the court of King Cyrus of Persia. Daniel, who was the only one who could explain the King's ominous dreams, is his most important advisor and confidant.

In the temple, there is a great idol of Bel, of which you can only see the legs in the painting. The King wants everyone to kneel before the statue, but Daniel refuses to do so. He only wants to kneel for a living God, not for an idol. 'But,' says the King, 'Bel is alive! Every night he eats the food we offer him.' When Daniel answers that bronze statues don't eat, he sees a suspicious look on the face of one of the priests. 'What's going on here?' Daniel wonders. To solve the mystery, he scatters a film of ash on the temple floor at night. The following morning, the priests' footprints in the ash reveal the truth.

Do you think it's easy for Daniel to refuse the King's order?

Saint Bartholomew (1661)
One of Rembrandt's friends or neighbors may have posed as the model for Saint Bartholomew. If we didn't know the name of the painting, it would just seem like a portrait of a thoughtful old man, with a long life behind him.

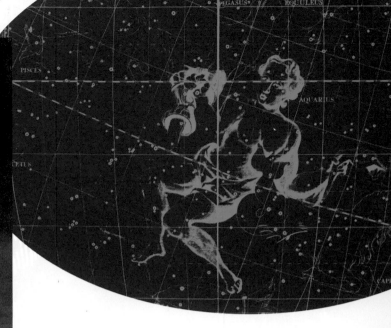

The star sign Aquarius

Is the bird flying very high with the boy? How do you know how high it's flying?

Can you see what the light is shining on?

The Abduction of Ganymede (1635) a story about the Greek gods

What is that big eagle doing high up in the sky? He has kidnapped Prince Ganymede in his big claws. The boy is crying and struggling against the eagle. He does not want to be carried away by the scary bird. He is so scared he wets himself. The bird carries him away to Mount Olympus. That's the mountain where the Greek gods live. The gods think that Ganymede is a beautiful and lovely boy. They very much want him to live with them.

But the eagle is no ordinary eagle. He is Zeus, the big boss of all the Greek gods. And Zeus has his own plans for the boy. He wants Ganymede to live forever. So he changes the prince into the star sign Aquarius. Ganymede will sparkle forever in the heavens. And as rainmaker he will give water to the world.

Ganymede was always shown as a beautiful, brave child. But not by Rembrandt! He could imagine that the boy must have been very frightened.

Zeus, the Supreme God

Rembrandt, from young boy...

This self-portrait was painted in1629.

1 — 23 years old

2 — 24 years old

3 — 24 years old

8 — 28 years old

9 — 28 years old

10 — 33 years old

11 — 34 years old

16 — 52 years old

17 — 53 years old

18 — 54 years old

19 — 55 years old

Rembrandt closely studied his own face. He painted 80 portraits of it. He looks different in each portrait. In one, he looks at you laughing. In others, he looks shocked or serious or angry. He sometimes wore beautiful costumes and pretended to be a king or a soldier. You can see Rembrandt getting older in the portraits.

...to old man

24 years old

25 years old

26 years old

28 years old

36 years old

about 38 years old

46 years old

49 years old

55 - 63 years old

63 years old

63 years old

This is the last Self-Portrait Rembrandt ever made

Fill in. In which self-portrait do you think Rembrandt:

looks sad	number…	looks like a learned man	number…
looks cheerful	number…	looks tired	number…
looks surprised	number…	looks just like a king	number…
looks like a real artist	number…	has concealed his eyes	number…

25

Get busy!

Painting in the dark

You will need: a friend, a room you can make dark, a flashlight or small lamp, thick drawing paper, paint and paintbrushes.

Make the room dark by closing the curtains. If the room is not dark enough then hang a blanket or a sheet in front of the window. Get your friend to sit on a chair. Shine the lamp on his or her face from all directions. Can you see the face changing? It may sometimes look scary. Shine the light on the part of the face you think looks best. Position the lamp so that it cannot fall down. Then paint your friend. Pay close attention to where the light shines on the face of your friend. Make those places light in your painting. Make the places where the shadow falls dark.

Your best story...

You will need: a big sheet of colored paper, sheets of drawing and writing paper, scissors and glue, colored pencils, paint and paintbrushes.

Rembrandt read a lot of stories. He painted pictures about the stories. Do you also know a good story? An exciting, funny or romantic story that you have read or made up yourself? Write it down. Choose the most important part of the story. Make a drawing or painting about it. Finish it by drawing a nice frame around it.

Glue your framed drawing and your story onto the sheet of colored paper. You can add small drawings or photos and draw frames around them too.

Have you changed a lot?

Rembrandt is famous for his self-portraits. Have you ever made a self-portrait yourself? These days, we do not paint many portraits. We do take a lot of photos though. Do you have any photos of yourself as a baby or when you were a toddler? Try to find photos of yourself for each year of your life. From when you were just born, or when you were 1 or 2 years old, 3, 4 and so on. Put them in the right order. Have you changed much?

You can paste the photos in a scrapbook or album. Write your age under each photo. Perhaps you can remember something about when the photo was made. You could write that next to the photo. If you keep the scrapbook or album, you can add a new photo of yourself each year.

Here you can paste small drawings or photos about your story

My best story

Make a nice frame of paper to frame your painting or drawing

Paste your story next to your drawing on a big sheet of colored paper

Head over heels in love

Saskia van Uylenburgh (1612 - 1642)

Saskia came from a wealthy and distinguished family that lived in Friesland. Her father was a mayor. Her mother died when she was only six years old. A few years later she was sent to live with her uncle Hendrick in Amsterdam. Later still, when her father died, Saskia came into a large inheritance.

Rembrandt meets Saskia

Rembrandt was working in his studio in the house of Hendrick van Uylenburg. One morning, a young woman walked in. Rembrandt immediately forgot everything around him. 'What a beautiful woman! Who is she?' It was Saskia, Hendrick's niece. It was love at first sight, and Rembrandt only had eyes for her. He wanted to marry her.

It wasn't every day that a miller's son got the chance to marry the daughter of an important family. Even so, Saskia's family were pleased with Rembrandt. The young painter was becoming more and more famous and he was earning good money.

Rembrandt was proud of his beautiful wife. He wanted nothing better than to draw her and to paint her. He drew this portrait of her, so that even when she was not there he could still look at her. Saskia has a dreamy look in the drawing. Is she thinking about Rembrandt?

Special materials

Rembrandt noted about this drawing: 'I made this portrait of my wife when she was twenty-one years old, three days after we were engaged to be married, on 8 June 1633.'

Rembrandt made a very special drawing. He used silverpoint on parchment. Silverpoint drawings are made using a thin silver rod that has been sharpened at one end, rather like a pencil. Parchment is a type of leather made from the skin of a lamb or a calf. The skin is first made very smooth and then treated with a special oil. Only then can you draw on it.

**RIDDLE:
When did Rembrandt make this drawing? It was not 8 June 1633.**

Were Rembrandt and Saskia already married when he made this drawing?

Saskia as Flora (1635)

Saskia made Rembrandt so happy that he painted her as his Flora. Flora was the Roman goddess of the spring and the flowers. That's why Rembrandt painted Saskia with so many flowers in this picture. She looks very contented. She has put on her finest dress for this painting. A graceful dress embroidered with golden thread. She's wearing some fine transparent lace that you can just see around her face. It is almost invisible.

You can vaguely see some leaves in the dark background. Is she walking in a forest? She is resting in the spring sunshine. Can you see the shadows of the flowers in her hand falling on her dress?

Can you see where Flora is adorned with even more flowers and twigs?

Do you think that Flora is looking right at you?

Rembrandt probably used Saskia as a model quite often. He let her play many different historical roles. We are not always sure whether it really is Saskia. Compare the drawing of Saskia with the painting of Flora. What do you think? Is it her, or not?

Which colors did Rembrandt use for Flora's dress?

Here come the Civil Guards!

The civil guards patrolled the city walls every day. That way they could keep an eye on the city. In earlier times, their task was to protect the city. But later, in the Golden Age, their job was mainly to show themselves off. The civil guards enjoyed giving big parties. That's why they had a new banqueting hall built. And to create a real party atmosphere, they wanted the walls to be decorated with paintings. They chose six painters to do these paintings. Rembrandt was one of them.

A bit of a mess

It was busy in his studio. Rembrandt was working on the Night Watch. It was to be his biggest painting, measuring some 16 by 13 feet. There were going to be at least sixteen civil guards in the painting.

A few civil guards had brought their finest costumes and weapons. But Rembrandt had other ideas. He asked them to wear their oldest helmets and carry their oldest weapons. He did not want to make an ordinary group portrait in which everyone stood in a row in all their finery. Like in a school photo, in which you could see everyone equally well.

It looks as if the civil guards have all just turned up and are chatting and standing around. But Rembrandt is playing games with us. He invented this jumble of people himself. He didn't feel sixteen civil guards made it quite crowded enough, so he added a few more people.

To get a place in the Night Watch, you had to pay. This was not a problem for the rich officers, but it was for the ordinary civil guards. The captain and the lieutenant paid more than a hundred guilders for their portrait. That was a lot of money in the Golden Age. That's why they got the main role in the painting. They're standing right at the front, in the middle of the light. And it looks as if they could step right out of the painting.

Rembrandt shows you how to use a gun

1 *The civil guard in the red suit is loading his weapon with gunpowder.*

2 *Behind the captain, a young man is shooting his gun in the air.*

3 *Another civil guard is blowing the remaining gunpowder from his gun.*

The Night Watch (1642)

The drummer is announcing the group with a drum roll. A dog is barking at him. The musketeers are standing at the gate, all ready to leave. There is a buzz of excitement in the air. Nobody knows where to stand yet. The sergeant with the black hat and the white collar shows one of the musketeers his place. Captain Banning Cocq is walking at the front in a black suit with a red sash. He tells Lieutenant Ruytenburgh to order the men to march.

A small boy is running ahead of the group. In his hand he's carrying a gunpowder horn with gunpowder for the muskets. He can't see much. His big helmet has fallen over his eyes.

And who is that standing out above everyone else? It's the man with the flag. You can't miss him! At the back in the dark are the pikemen. Their sharp and dangerous pikes are pointing in all directions. Do you see the little girl in the golden yellow dress? She is selling food and drink.

Painters often included themselves in this sort of painting. They chose a place where they wouldn't stand out. Rembrandt put himself in this painting twice. Can you see him?

The captain is wearing only one glove. Can you find his other glove?

The civil guards had three symbols: a gun, a bird's claw and oak leaves. Can you find any of these in the painting?

There's another girl hidden amongst the men. Can you see where she is?

Not true...

It's often said that the civil guards weren't at all pleased with the Night Watch. Some even say they hid the painting in a dark attic. But that's not true. The Night Watch hung on the wall of the banqueting hall for more than half a century.

A wizard with light

Do you also feel that Rembrandt's paintings have something mysterious about them? Rembrandt was a wizard with light. He always made the light shine on the most important parts of the painting. That's where the colors start to glow. And then from the deep darkness people just seem to appear. It's all so cleverly done that you forget the light is painted; it's like magic.

Why the Night Watch was made smaller

In 1715, the Night Watch was moved to the Town Hall. The painting was just a bit too big. Strips were taken from the top and from the left side, cutting off two of the civil guards. The Night Watch now measures about 14 x 12 feet.

The painting's nickname

The painting was not always called the Night Watch. Because the painting had become so dark, people thought it showed the civil guards on duty at night. That's why, around 1800, people started to call the painting the Night Watch.

Sunday 14 September 1975: unknown man slashes 'The Night Watch'

At one o'clock, when the Rijksmuseum in Amsterdam opened, a tall, inconspicuous man entered the building with the other visitors. With long strides he walked to the room where the Night Watch was on display. He stood still for a moment.

Suddenly, he ran towards the Night Watch. The museum attendant called out, "Sir, you can't go so close to the painting!" But it was too late. Before the museum attendant could do anything, the unknown man had pulled a knife and made twelve big cuts in the Night Watch. It was all over at precisely three minutes past one. The museum attendant and a visitor tried to drag the man away from the painting. The man dropped the knife on the floor. He had used so much force the knife was completely buckled. Other attendants came running when they heard the noise. The man was taken away.

The Night Watch had been damaged so much that a whole piece had fallen out on the floor. Curious visitors quickly filled the room. They couldn't believe their eyes and stared at the damaged painting in shock.

Major restoration

Fortunately, the painting could be repaired. The restoration work was immediately started the next morning. The restorers were worried that pieces of the Night Watch might come off. So for the time being they stuck them on the back of the painting with sticky tape. The old painting needed a lot of restoration. The varnish had become so dark that you could almost no longer see the colors of the painting.

The restoration was going to take about five months. The painting was so big that it didn't fit into the restoration studio. So it was left hanging where it was in the museum. Restoration is a very precise job and requires a lot of patience. The restorers needed peace and quiet to be able to do their job properly. They worked behind a glass wall and closed curtains. At the end of every day the curtains were opened and you could see how they had got on.

Now that the restoration is finished you can't see any trace of the cuts in the canvas. And the colors look as good as new again, as if Rembrandt had painted the Night Watch only yesterday.

Get busy!

That's eye-catching!
Rembrandt used lots of dark colors in his paintings.
Only the main figures have been painted in
lighter colors.

This is how you make light and dark colors with paint.

You will need: white paper, water, paint, paintbrushes and a palette or plate to mix the paint on.

There are two ways to make light colors:

1. You can add a little white paint to the dark paint.

2. Or you can add more water, which makes the paint thinner. The white of the paper will then shine through the color of the paint.

You can make paint darker by adding a little black paint. Don't use too much water – that will make the color look gray.

Magic with light

You will need: 2 sheets of white paper, water, paintbox, paintbrushes, scissors and glue.

Paint a landscape in dark colors on one of the sheets of paper. You could paint a forest or mountains, or a jungle or a moonscape. Paint the other sheet with lots of different light colors so there's no more white showing. Cut out a few figures – people, animals or flowers – from your light-colored sheet and place them on your dark landscape. Move them around until you have found the right place for them. What is it that strikes you?

Thick paint

Rembrandt began to use thicker and thicker paint. If you look closely at his paintings, the paint looks rough and lumpy. Rembrandt not only used paintbrushes, but also the wooden part of his paintbrush, an ordinary brush and even his fingers!

Drawing in a thick layer of paint

You will need: thick paper or cardboard, thick paint and paintbrushes.

Paint a background of bright colors, such as red, orange or yellow. Let the paint dry. Spread a thick layer of paint in one color on it. Now scratch a drawing in it with the stick of your paintbrush. Allow the paint to dry thoroughly.

Paint a portrait in thick paint

You will need: acrylic paint, paintbrushes, thick paper, plates, sand, pieces of seashell, finely crushed eggshells, tiny beads or stones and seeds. Perhaps you can think of other things to use.

You can make thick paint by mixing it with all sorts of things. Choose a few colors. Mix one of the things listed above into one of the colors. That way you end up with different sorts of thick paint. Now think up a face and make a portrait of it. Use your imagination. Choose the type of paint you think fits best with the various parts of the face – the hair, the nose and the mouth and so on.

Big changes

A son at last...

Saskia lying sick in bed, only thirty years old (1640)

While Rembrandt was busy painting The Night Watch, his son Titus was born. Saskia and Rembrandt were not very lucky. Their first three children had only lived for a few weeks. You can imagine how happy they were when Titus turned out to be a healthy child. But Saskia was not very well. Every time Rembrandt came home, he found her sitting exhausted in a chair or lying sick in bed. In Rembrandt's paintings of the time, Saskia looks old and tired. Nine months after Titus was born, she died. Now Rembrandt had to take care of Titus on his own. And he also had to take care of his pupils who lived in his house.

Titus

Rembrandt wanted to teach Titus how to draw and paint. But Titus didn't have his father's talent. Not one of his paintings has survived. But he was a good art dealer. That would be very useful to Rembrandt later.

When Saskia died she left a lot of money to Titus in her will. But Rembrandt, who was in charge of the money, spent it all. That's why Titus never got a single penny of his inheritance.

In spite of this, Titus was a friendly boy and always ready to help his father. One day, when Rembrandt was short of money again, he had to sell a mirror that had a very expensive frame. To surprise his father, Titus bought it back with his own savings. But on his way home, the mirror broke into a hundred thousand pieces. Titus wasn't very lucky either.

Titus at a writing desk, 1655

The kitchen

A new woman in Rembrandt's life

*I*n the summer of 1649, Hendrickje Stoffels came to live in Rembrandt's house as a housemaid. She became good friends with Titus. Rembrandt couldn't keep his eyes off the pretty girl. She was twenty years younger than he was. They didn't get married, but they did have a daughter.

Living with Rembrandt wasn't always easy for Hendrickje. Although Rembrandt couldn't complain about the amount of work he was asked to do, he just didn't know how to handle money. The problems started when he couldn't pay his bills anymore. He had to sell his beautiful big house on the Jodenbreestraat. But Hendrickje didn't leave him.

Hendrickje and Titus rented a little house on the Rozengracht. They opened a shop and sold paintings and antiques to earn some money. This meant Rembrandt could go on painting. They gave him enough to eat and drink, but they didn't give him any money. Hendrickje stayed with Rembrandt until she died.

Woman Bathing in a Stream (1654)

The woman is standing on the banks of a stream. She really wants to have a bath! She looks around her. 'Good, I'm all alone,' she thinks. But is she? We can see her, can't we? The woman slips her beautiful red gown off her shoulders and lays it at the side of the stream. She doesn't want her petticoat to get wet. So she lifts it up. She carefully steps into the cold water. She smiles when she sees her face reflected in the water.

Rembrandt has given her a smooth skin in his painting. Just like the surface of the water. The rough fabric of the linen petticoat is painted very differently. You can see it is painted in broad brushstrokes.

Rembrandt probably used Hendrickje as his model here. The same woman appears in other paintings. But he never put her name on it. So we can only guess that it is Hendrickje.

Do you see where the red gown is reflected in the water?

TRICK QUESTION: Does water feel hard or soft? And what about the water in the painting?

Soft or hard, smooth or rough?

When you stroke a stone or a piece of fabric, you immediately feel the difference between them. The stone feels hard and the fabric feels soft. Soft materials should look soft on paintings. Look how Rembrandt managed to do this.

Draw what you feel

You will need: a cloth, different objects, drawing paper and pencils.
Ask someone to put some things under a cloth. Things that are soft or hard, smooth or rough. Put your hand under the cloth. Touch one of the things. Don't look at it. With your other hand, draw what you feel.

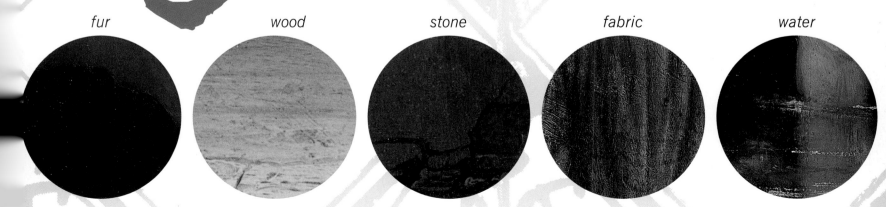

fur   wood   stone   fabric   water

Rich but still poor

Fooled

Rembrandt earned a lot of money. He was paid well for his etchings and paintings and his pupils had to pay apprenticeship fees. He also earned money by selling their work. And… he was a dealer in other painters' art. Yet he never had enough money.

A sculpture from the times of the Greek writer Homer

Houbraken recounts: His pupils soon discovered that Rembrandt was greedy. So they liked to play tricks on him. They painted a penny on the floor of his studio. When Rembrandt tried to pick it up, the pupils laughed amongst themselves. They had fooled him again. Rembrandt didn't say a thing because he was a bit embarrassed.

Where did all Rembrandt's money go? He lived modestly. He was quite happy to live on bread and cheese. But Rembrandt was addicted to art and beautiful things. When he saw something beautiful, he just had to buy it. So he spent more than he earned. And he ran up a lot of debts. That's why Rembrandt had to sell not only his house, but also all the beautiful things he had collected. It made him very unhappy. In 1658, he moved to a small house on the Rozengracht.

Rembrandt's house
The big, elegant house on the Jodenbreestraat in Amsterdam is still there. It's now a museum that you can visit.

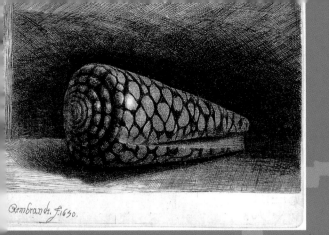

Rembrandt. f. 1630.

List of possessions

Rembrandt was forced to sell his house and all his possessions. A list was made of everything he owned. The rooms were crammed full of his things. Look at what he had on the ground floor of his house.

Can you find the room where he kept the old sculptures from ancient Greek and Roman times?

Rembrandt drew many of the things he had collected. You can find some of these things on the inside of the covers of this book. Can you find out what he used as a model for the etching of the shell and the drawing of the birds of paradise?

Can you also find the things he used for the Night Watch?

Have you got a collection too?

If you have, choose the item you like best. Make a drawing of it, just like Rembrandt did. You can also draw something from Rembrandt's collection.

The hall

Paintings by Rembrandt:
- 3 historical paintings
- 4 portraits,
- 1 landscape
- 1 painting with animals
- 1 etching by Rembrandt of a funeral • 6 paintings by other Dutch and Flemish painters and 3 by Italian painters • 3 antique sculptures from ancient times a tablecloth • 6 chairs with blue seats • a chair with a cane seat a bed • 2 pillows • 2 blankets blue wallpaper • a large mirror a large cupboard

The printing press room

Paintings by Rembrandt:
3 historical paintings, 1 figure painting, 1 portrait • copies of paintings by Rembrandt:
27 paintings by other Dutch and Flemish painters and 2 by Italian painters • an oak table 4 old chairs in bad condition 4 green chair cushions • 1 copper kettle • a hatstand

The corridor

A book with sketches of figures by Rembrandt some old chairs 9 white dishes 2 plates

The side room

Paintings by Rembrandt:
- 3 historical paintings
- 3 figure paintings - 3 portraits
5 landscapes - 1 painting with animals - 1 still-life
- 18 paintings by other Dutch painters - 3 paintings by Italian painters • a mirror in an expensive ebony frame

The vestibule

Paintings by Rembrandt: a woman with a child, a standing woman, St. Jerome, a soldier at arms 3 portraits and a self-portrait 8 small landscapes • a painting with hares, a pig and fighting lions • 10 paintings by other Dutch and Flemish painters 3 sculptures of children 1 plaster bust

A plan of the ground floor of Rembrandt's house

Rembrandt the etcher

picture, two pictures and thousands more...

*T*hese days, making thousands of copies of a picture with a printing press is nothing special. Posters, postcards, stickers – we can easily make lots of copies. In the Golden Age, they didn't have machines for printing. But they did have a way of making copies of a picture. If you made an etching, you could print one hundred copies of the drawing. And in those days, that was a lot of copies. How etchings are made is explained on page 48.

Rembrandt, famous for his etchings

Rembrandt made many etchings. His etchings were very popular. Art collectors from all over Europe not only bought his latest print – they also wanted all the other prints, even if Rembrandt had only changed the etching very slightly. Because you can make a hundred prints from one etching, Rembrandt's etchings were cheaper than his paintings.

*An etching needle and
etching plate*

Not satisfied with the first state

The first print of your etching is called the first 'state'. If you're not satisfied with your etching then you can change the drawing on the plate. The next print you make is called the second 'state'. You can repeat this process over and over again.

The 'first state' of The Pancake Woman

The 'second state' of The Pancake Woman

The Pancake Woman (1635)

An old woman is making three pancakes in a large pan. One of the boys has just bought a pancake from her and is taking a large bite out of it. The other boys would like a pancake too. The little boy in the front doesn't want to share his pancake with anyone else. Can you see the danger lurking?

Rembrandt thought the old woman didn't stand out enough among the children. He decided to change that. He made her darker with a few fine lines. She now catches the eye much more.

Can you see the black cat looking at the little dog?

How many children can you see in the etching?

How an etching is made

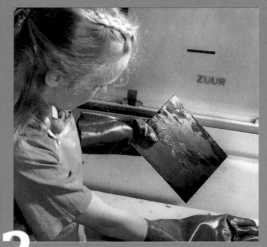

1 You first coat a metal plate with wax or varnish. With an etching needle, you scratch a drawing in the soft layer. By doing this you partly scratch away some of the soft layer.

2 You must then put the plate in an acid bath. Where you have scratched away the soft layer, the acid etches grooves in the metal plate.

3 After you have cleaned the plate, you can see that the drawing has been etched into the plate. You fill the grooves with ink by rubbing oily printing ink into the plate.

Different shades of gray in Rembrandt's etchings

From light gray to dark gray

You will need: 1 black pencil

Try to make 8 different shades of gray in the boxes below with a black pencil. By filling a box with diagonal lines it will become gray. The more lines, the darker the gray becomes. Try to make the first box very light gray. Make each box a little darker than the one before it. Then you'll get 8 different shades of gray.

example

light gray → → → → *slightly darker gray* → → → →*a little bit darker again...*→ → →

4 Now the ink must be wiped off the smooth plate. To get the plate really clean, you can wipe it with your hand. But you have to make sure the grooves stay filled with ink.

5 Then you lay a sheet of paper on the plate. The plate and paper are pressed together in a heavy printing press. The ink from the grooves is printed onto the paper by the pressure of the press.

6 When you take the paper off the plate, you can see the drawing.

Too many prints made

A number of Rembrandt's etching plates have been preserved. They were used to make prints up until the beginning of the 20th century. These prints are not as good as the ones made earlier. If you make too many prints, the plate wears out. The fine lines disappear and the image becomes a bit fuzzy.

The plate and the etching (1636)

On the left you can see one of Rembrandt's etching plates with five portraits of Saskia and an old woman. Next to it is the print that was made from the plate. Can you see that the print is a mirror image of what is on the plate?

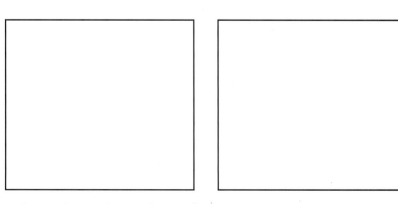

and darker again… → → → →   and darker again… → → → →   dark gray

This is the first state of an etching by Rembrandt

The Angel Appearing to the Shepherds (1634)

It's a dark night. The shepherds are in the fields guarding their flocks. Suddenly, a bright light appears in the sky. Most of the shepherds and the animals run away. Some of them are frozen to the spot, rigid with fear. Then an angel appears, surrounded by cherubs. The angel tells the shepherds that Jesus will be born in a stable in Nazareth.

How many shepherds can you see?

Two shepherds are coming out from their hiding place. Can you see them?

Is it the night before or after Christmas?

What can you see between the angels in the middle of the bright light?

Never tired of working on it.

Rembrandt was almost never satisfied with the first print of an etching. He would scratch away what he didn't like. Or he added a new layer of wax and continued to work on the plate. He never tired of working on it. No other artist could make so many shades of black and gray as he did in his etchings. We still haven't worked out exactly how he managed this.

2 *This is the second state of the same etching.*

Spot the difference between the two etchings.
Mark the circles with a cross: in which etching...

	1 the first state	2 the second state
• can you see the trees and the bushes best?	◯	◯
• can you see lighter areas with sketches of animals and angels?	◯	◯
• does the big angel stand out most?	◯	◯
• can you see most angels?	◯	◯
• did Rembrandt use most shades of black and gray?	◯	◯
• can you see a town in the distance?	◯	◯

Rembrandt the draughtsman

Drawing outdoors

Rembrandt didn't always work in his studio. He often went for long walks in the countryside around Amsterdam. His pupils sometimes came along. They all had a sketchbook with them. They would walk out of the city along the river Amstel. On their way they made sketches of the open landscape. They could see ditches, farms and mills far into the distance. The pupils gasped in amazement when their master sketched the landscape in just a few lines. They wished they could draw that well too.

Because the city was expanding fast, a lot of building was going on around Amsterdam. If Rembrandt thought a building or church tower didn't fit in his drawing, he just left it out.

When everyone was tired and hungry after a long day in the fresh air, they went to an inn to have something to eat and drink.

Drawing black lines

You will need: as many different kinds of black drawing materials as you can find (such as pencils, chalk, wax crayons, felt-tips and pens) and paper. Draw lines on the paper from left to right with all your different pens and pencils. Can you see that all the lines are different? Some of them have sharp edges and others are a bit ragged. You can use these differences very well in a drawing. To draw the woollen coat of a sheep, for example, you could use a soft pencil or crayon. That makes the sheep's coat look softer. And if you want to draw a stone, it's better to use a hard pencil or a pen.

Lots of lines or not many lines. Rembrandt made these two drawings of farms that were situated on a bend in the river Amstel. Compare the two drawings. Which drawing took him the longest to do? How can you tell?

Drawing outdoors, just like Rembrandt

You will need: as many different kinds of black drawing materials as you can find (such as pencils, chalk, wax crayons, felt-tips and pens) and a sketchbook.

When the weather's good, it's fun to draw outdoors. Take your drawing materials and sketchbook with you and find a nice spot, in a town or in the country. Draw a picture of your surroundings using only black drawing materials, just like Rembrandt did. Why not draw outdoors when you're on holiday? Then you'll have a nice souvenir to take home.

Three women and a child at the door

Drawing without lifting your pencil

You will need: a pencil and paper

Draw a face with a pencil, but don't lift your pencil from the paper. Try pressing a little harder in some places and a little softer in others. Can you see the difference?

The last big commission (1662-1663)

In Amsterdam, all black and blue woolen cloth had to be inspected. This important job was done by the Syndics. If the cloth was well woven, and nice and smooth, the Syndics would give it their approval. To show the cloth had been inspected and approved, they would attach a lead seal to it. Cloth without a lead seal was worthless.

After many years, Rembrandt was finally given a big commission to paint again. This time it was a group portrait of the Syndics. Rembrandt was not allowed to choose the composition of his painting entirely himself. The Syndics wanted to be portrayed sitting at the table. And their servant was to stand behind them. Rembrandt was also told how big the painting should be. But Rembrandt wouldn't be Rembrandt if he hadn't tried to put his own ideas into the painting.

The Syndics have gathered in their stately workroom for a meeting. They don't have to inspect cloth today. The big book is lying open on the table, which is covered with a red Persian rug. The governor is sitting in the middle. The servant is standing with his back to the wood-paneled wall, calmly watching them. The Syndics are just about to start their meeting. Are they looking up because you have suddenly entered the room?

Who is who?

The men in The Syndics are from left to right: Jacob van Loon, Folckert Jansz., Willem van Doeyenburg, the servant Frans Bel, Arnout van der Meye and Jochem de Neve.

Hung high

Rembrandt knew that the painting would be hung high up on the wall. He took this into account when he painted the group portrait. You look up to the men from below. It looks as if Rembrandt has put the men onto a stage.

56

This is an X-ray of The Syndics. It shows you layers of paint that would otherwise be invisible.

Are you a good detective?

When Rembrandt started a new painting, he didn't make any sketches beforehand. He already knew what he wanted to paint. Being able to paint directly onto the canvas without a sketch was something only great painters could do. He often changed things in the painting while he was working on it. You can see those changes in the X-ray.

You can even see the nails that attach the canvas to the frame. Try comparing the X-ray to the painting.

The chairman's head
At first Rembrandt didn't know the direction in which he wanted the chairman to look. In the X-ray it's just as if the chairman has three heads. Can you see it too?

The chairman's hand
Rembrandt changed the chairman's hand three times. Can you see the different positions of the hand?

Half standing, half sitting
Folckert Jansz. was at first painted standing up. But that's not what the Syndics wanted. So Rembrandt painted him as if he is just about to sit down. Can you see that Folckert was first painted standing up in the X-ray?

The Jewish Bride

59

Red, gold and glowing colors

*I*n the autumn of 1885, the painter Vincent van Gogh wrote the following about The Jewish Bride (1665): 'Really, I'd be happy to give ten years of my life for the chance to spend a fortnight sitting in front of this picture, surviving on a crust of dry bread.'

Vincent van Gogh was not the only one who was fascinated by this painting. Many artists tried to find out how Rembrandt painted The Jewish Bride. He didn't only use his paintbrush, but he also used a palette knife, the handle of his paintbrush and a normal brush. He even used his fingers to mould the thick layer of paint into the right shape.

But it is still a mystery. The picture is painted so roughly that you can only see thick daubs of paint when you look at it closely. Yet from a distance, everything falls into place. It no longer looks like paint – hands, sleeves, fabric and soft skin all make their appearance. The man tenderly lays his hand on the breast of the woman. It is obvious that they love each other.

hand	sleeve	fabric	skin

Thick layers of paint

There were only a few painters who painted pictures with thick layers of paint like Rembrandt. It made people curious. They wanted to take a close look at his paintings. But Rembrandt didn't want them to look so close. He would pull them away from the painting and say, 'the smell of the paint will bother you'. It was sometimes even said about Rembrandt's later portraits that you could pick them up by the nose.

page .....   page .....   page .....   page .....

page .....   page .....   page .....   page .....

Can you find these faces in the book?
Write the right page number next to each face.

Still not forgotten

In the period shortly before Rembrandt died, it was quiet in Rembrandt's house. He didn't care what other people thought of him. He only painted what he wanted to paint, even when he hardly sold any paintings. He hadn't had any pupils for years. Rembrandt and his daughter Cornelia hardly had any money to buy food. He once even had to break open her piggybank. His house was furnished with cheap furniture. But Rembrandt needed three rooms to store his art collection!

Yet the painter was not forgotten. His work was well-known throughout Europe. In 1667 he was even visited by Cosimo de' Medici from Italy. The Italian called Rembrandt 'pittore famoso', the famous painter.

Rembrandt died on 4 October 1669. He wasn't honored with the big funeral that you would expect such a great painter to receive.

Rembrandt still makes the news

There are a number of paintings which we're still not sure about; did Rembrandt really paint them or not? Some copies that were made by Rembrandt's pupils have been sold as real 'Rembrandts'. And some of his pupils' own paintings, the ones that were painted in exactly the same style as their master's, have also been sold as real 'Rembrandts'. Sometimes Rembrandt even put his signature on these paintings. But later other people did that too. If only Rembrandt had made a list of all his works. Then we would know exactly which paintings are his.

Whenever a fake Rembrandt is discovered again, the art world is in uproar. So Rembrandt still knows how to make the news!

Self-portrait in oriental costume, Rembrandt, 1613

Copy of Rembrandt in oriental costume, by a pupil

Real or fake

These two paintings look very similar. Can you see the difference? The painting on the left shows Rembrandt with a poodle, but there is no poodle in the other painting. An X-ray has shown that Rembrandt added the poodle later. One of his pupils had copied Rembrandt's painting before the dog had been painted in. That's how we know that the painting on the left is the real Rembrandt.

Illustrations

Bibliography

- Holm Bevers, Peter Schatborn and Barbara Welzel, *Rembrandt: The Master and His Workshop: Drawings and Etchings*, New Haven: Yale University Press, 1991

- Christopher Brown, Jan Kelch, Pieter van Thiel, *Rembrandt: The Master and His Workshop: Paintings*, New Haven: Yale University Press, 1991

- Bob Haak, *Rembrandt: His Life, Work and Times*, The Hague

- Gary Schwartz, *Rembrandt*, Amsterdam, 1994

- Christian Tümpel, *Rembrandt*, Nijmegen, 1992

- Ernst van de Wetering, *Rembrandt, The Painter at Work*, Amsterdam, 1997

- Exhibition catalogue, *Rembrandt 1669/1969*, Amsterdam, 1969

Colophon

Concept, text, illustrations, graphic design: Ceciel de Bie and Martijn Leenen, Amsterdam

Cover illustration: Majel, Amsterdam

Consultants: Michiel Franken and Sjraar van Heugten, Amsterdam

Translation: Baxter Associates, Hilversum

Lithography: Fritz Repro BV, Almere

Printer: Snoeck-Ducaju & Zoon, Gent, Belgium

Publisher: Original published by V + K Publishing, Blaricum, in cooperation with The Rembrandthuis, Amsterdam

Answers

Page 8
Rembrandt is 23 years old in this painting.

There are holes in the legs of the easel. You can put the sticks on which the painting rests in these holes. For a large painting, you put the sticks in the holes lower down, for a small painting you put them in the holes higher up.

The floor is made of wood.

There are pots on the table.

Rembrandt is wearing a painter's coat to protect his clothes. And, of course, without heating, it can get very cold in the studio in winter.

There is a door behind the easel to the right.

Page 17
Nicolaes doesn't look very cheerful. But if you think he looks angry, serious or friendly, these are all correct answers.

Yes, Nicolaes is looking straight at you.

His hand is resting on a red chair.

Nicolaes is wearing an expensive fur coat and an expensive fur hat. He looks very smart with his nice white collar.

Page 22
By his clothes; he stands in the light, holding a staff in his hand; and the King is very big.

In the cup and dish on the table.

You can see the face of one of the priests on the left, in the dark, hidden behind Daniel.

No, he hardly dares to look at the King.

Page 23
The bird isn't flying very high yet. You can still see the outline of a building and some trees.

The light is shining on Ganymede.

Page 25
If you looked carefully, then all your answers are correct.

Page 29
The drawing was made on 11 June 1633. No, Rembrandt and Saskia were engaged to be married when Rembrandt made the drawing.

Page 31
Flora is wearing a flower garland on her head. The walking stick is decorated with leaves. And she's wearing a necklace with flowers.

Flora isn't quite looking straight at you. It looks as though she's looking just past you.

Rembrandt painted Flora's dress in light and soft colors. Light yellow, soft green, gold and cream.

It probably is Saskia. She looks very much like the drawing that Rembrandt made of her.

Page 35
He's holding the other glove with the same hand.

The girl with the yellow dress has a chicken hanging by its feet from her belt. The boy in the middle has oak leaves on his helmet. Three of the men are busy with their guns.

The other girl is behind the girl with the yellow dress. If you look very carefully, you can just see her head.

Page 43
In the left-hand corner of the painting you can see the reflection of the red dress in the water.

TRICK QUESTION
When you do a belly flop on the water it feels very hard. When you put your hand in the water it feels very soft. And… when it's frozen it feels like stone!
The water in the painting looks very soft.

Page 45
The antique sculptures are in the hall.

You'll find the shell at the back of the book.

The stuffed bird of paradise is at the front of the book.
For the Night Watch he used the helmet which you can find at the front of the book and the pikes you can find at the back.

Page 47
The dog would also like some of the boy's pancake.

There are seven children.

Yes, in the bottom right of the picture you can see the black cat looking at the little dog.

Page 50-51
Spot the differences:
You can see the trees and the bushes best in etching 2.
You can see lighter areas with sketches of animals and angels in etching 1.
The big angel stands out most in etching 2.
Etching 2 shows most angels.
Rembrandt used most shades of black and gray in etching 2.
You can see a town in the distance in etching 1.

There are 6 shepherds in the etching.

It's Christmas Eve. The angels are telling the shepherds that Jesus will be born the next day.

On the right you can see the shepherds coming out of their hiding places.

There is a dove in the middle of the bright light in between the angels.

Page 52
Rembrandt probably spent more time doing the drawing on the left. He has drawn in lots of very fine lines.

Page 61
You find the faces on the following pages:
Upper row: 20, 42, 54, 30
Lower row: 23, 18, 16, 24